Following God's Call

Scripture Meditations for Vocation Discernment

Judette A. Gallares, r.c.

A Copublication

of the

Cenacle
Quezon City, Philippines

and

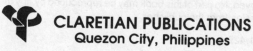

CLARETIAN PUBLICATIONS
Quezon City, Philippines

Claretian Publications is a pastoral endeavor of the Claretian Missionaries in the Philippines. It aims to promote a renewed spirituality rooted in the process of total liberation and solidarity in response to the needs, challenges and pastoral demands of the Church today.

The Scriptural quotations that appear in this book are from the *Christian Community Bible: Catholic Pastoral Edition* (Manila, Philippines: Claretian Publications, St. Paul Publications, and Divine Word Publications, 1988).

Published 1990 by The Religious of the Cenacle, Philippine Province, 59 Nicanor Reyes St., Loyola Heights, Quezon City 1108 AND Claretian Publications, U.P. P.O. Box 4, Quezon City 1101, Philippines.

Cover Design by Joseph Abando

ISBN 971-501-429-1

Contents

Contents

Foreword

This project was conceived and started in Bethany, just outside Jerusalem while I was participating in the 1988 Israel Study Program offered by the Catholic Theological Union. It was a time of transition in my life. I had just finished a full and demanding involvement in the ministry and an eight-year assignment as Vocation and Pre-Novitiate Directress for the Cenacle Congregation in the Philippines which left me depleted of psychic and spiritual energies. There were some areas in my life that needed sorting out before I could project myself into possible ministries in the future. Through the encouragement of my mentor and spiritual director, Eloise Rosenblatt, R.S.M. and Carroll Stuhlmueller, C.P., one of my professors in the Biblical Spirituality Program, I began to undertake this project as a way of integrating my previous personal and ministerial experiences and as a process of reflecting on the giftedness of my experiences as a spiritual companion to others seeking the path to God.

After several years "accompanying" people in their faith journey, I feel I have been privileged to share in their joy of discovering a more personal and loving God and in their struggles to live out the demands of their newly awakened faith. The Word of God has been the true teacher, friend and companion in these journeys. I therefore hope that this "small" book of Scripture meditations will help as a guide to those who are still seeking to discover meaning and direction in their lives. In their journey, may they encounter God who is the only source of true meaning and may God's Word — Jesus — become their true home.

This book is divided into two parts. The first part, "Listening to God's Call," deals with the meaning of the word, "vocation." It introduces us to what discernment is and its relationship to prayer. The second part is on the "Constants in God's Call." It is designed to highlight the various themes in the Bible that are *constant in God's call.* Each succeeding chapter focuses on a specific vocational theme. It begins with a point for prayerful consideration and offers several Scripture meditations, reflection questions and added Biblical passages.

The Scripture meditations may be used by a retreat director as points for the retreatant's prayer or by individuals as guide to their daily reflection. In either case, it would be beneficial to those using these materials for their prayer to have a spiritual director who can be their companion and guide along their prayer path.

Keeping a prayer journal would also be a help since this will give them a better sense of the movement and flow of their prayer life and of the progress of or obstacles to their faith journey.

Lastly, the guiding notes for the Scripture passages are meant to help them get started on their prayer. Also, the reflection questions after the Scripture meditation are there to offer further help. These can also be used as signposts for group faith-sharing. However, if these guiding notes and reflection questions become distractions or obstacles to one's prayer, then they should be dropped. *What is more important is to allow God to speak directly to the person through Scripture.*

Feast of Our Lady of the Cenacle
26 May 1990

Introduction:

Listening to God's Call

Listening to God's Call

Vocation is a word that has often been used primarily to label a calling to the priesthood or the religious life. However, vocation in its broadest sense simply means "a calling." As such the term cannot be confined to the priesthood or to the religious life alone. The other states of being are as much a vocation as being a priest or a religious. Therefore, if vocation is "a calling," we must take time to listen to it so that we may know what and where we are meant to be.

As persons, we are called by the providential arrangement of circumstances, by the realities of life, by our own limitations and potentials, by the historical moment, and by our own emotional, intellectual and psychological needs. If one follows the teachings of the *abbas* and *ammas* of the desert and of the fathers and doctors of the Church in this regard, one comes to accept that a vocation is found in the providential arrangement of significant aspects of life and by the grace which we receive to make the best of these situations.[1]

---

[1] See *A Guide to Religious Ministries* (New York: The Catholic News Publishing Co., 1989), pp. 8-9.

The process of listening and sifting through the providential arrangement of significant aspects of one's life as well as the grace to seek the truth of one's situation and to determine the best true response to God's love is called "discernment."

Discerning the Call

In discerning one's call to the priesthood, religious life or to a religious ministry, it is extremely important to keep in mind that this particular vocation is primarily a calling to dedicate one's life to the service of God. As such, it is much different from just deciding to choose a particular career. It is not just a call to do anything, go anywhere, or become something, although these may be part of the response.[2] The process of discerning one's call is an effort — both human and Divine — to choose a state of being that expresses one's best response to God's providential care and love. As such, it can never be undertaken alone since it calls for the interaction of two persons — the person of the discerner and the Person of God. Thus, discernment is always within the context of one's personal relationship with God.

---

[2] *ibid.*, p. 9.

Prayer and Discernment

Prayer is at the heart of one's relationship with God. Prayer disposes the person to the reality of God's guiding and leading presence in one's life. Prayer enables one to know the Other through a dialogical relationship.

Thus, discernment cannot be divorced from prayer, otherwise it will not be a true one. Discernment is not something one acquires by simply learning methods and techniques, although these can be helpful tools in the process of discernment itself.

Discernment is, first of all, a gift one seeks daily in prayer. One learns to hear with one's heart Christ's voice, to know its tone, sometimes, even to know what he is going to say before He says it. Discernment is an invitation born out of an intimate friendship and union with the Lord. It is a gift that enables one to distinguish the leadings of the Holy Spirit.

Therefore, a person entering into a discernment process must, at least, have the seeds of faith within oneself. One must be convinced that prayer strengthens and deepens one's bond of friendship with God. One must also believe that prayer and faith give purpose and meaning to a life lived in dedication and commitment to God's service.

Praying God's Word

God's word in Sacred Scripture is an enduring sign of the Holy One's desire to be in constant communication with us. We must make an effort to *listen openly*. This is an important disposition in entering into dialogue with God. We must set aside our self-centered desires and biases in order to truly understand the meaning of God's word in our lives.

We are invited to *interact honestly* with God's word by interpreting it within the context of our life situation. Yet, we must also be mindful that God's sacred words in Scripture were originally written in a different language within a particular culture, time and place by persons with a totally different worldview than ours. It is important that we understand the context in which it was written. Instead of interpreting its meaning literally, we must simply listen to God's enduring message for us in our present context. Thus, our interpretation of God's word involves the meeting of two cultures and worldviews — our own and that which conditioned the Scripture we are using for prayer.

Praying God's word requires patience and trust. Given the complexity of our world and the limitation of human comprehension, we cannot always readily understand the meaning of God's word. This can create within us a feeling of discomfort, impatience or confusion. However, we must not give up easily, but *wait patiently* and *trust humbly* that in time, God will lead us to its meaning. The first act of prayer is God's, not ours. All God is asking from us is to dispose ourselves to the action of the Spirit and to acknowledge with humility that God is the One who acts in and through us. God is the One who enables us to respond in love and service.

There are many ways and methods of praying Scripture. In fact, many books and articles have been written about it. But, the simplest way to begin is to take a chosen or suggested passage and read it slowly and meditatively, pause at a word or phrase that has an impact on us, repeating it to ourselves with great reverence like a *mantra* until it finds a quiet center within us. Don't rush! Take time! Be yourself before God! In great simplicity—

LISTEN OPENLY,

INTERACT HONESTLY,

WAIT PATIENTLY and

TRUST HUMBLY.

Opening Meditation

To begin the prayer journey, take any of the following Scripture passages for meditation. Ask for the grace of OPENNESS TO GOD'S WORD and for the LIGHT to recognize and acknowledge the leadings of God's Spirit:

- **Isaiah 55:6-11...** "Seek Yahweh while he may be found; call to him while he is near..."

- **Wisdom 7:7-29...** "I prayed and understanding was given to me."

- **Proverbs 2:1-15** "...If you heed my words and value my commands...then you will understand the fear of Yahweh, and you will find the knowledge of God.

- **Psalm 25...** "Teach me your ways, O Lord; make me know your paths..."

- **Psalm 119:33-36...** "Incline my heart to follow your will and not my own selfish desire..."

- **Jeremiah 29:11-14...** "When you call on me, I will listen. You will seek me and find me when you search for me with all your heart."

- **Hebrews 3:7-14...** "Listen to what the Holy Spirit says..."

• Hebrews 4:11-13..."For the word of God is living and effective, sharper than any two-edged sword..."

Let my prayer rise like incense...

Scripture Meditations:

Constants in God's Call

Constants in God's Call

Introduction

In discerning our call to the religious life or to a Church ministry, the Bible provides us with images and characteristics of God that are constantly present in the Divine call. These are the aspects to which we must be attentive in testing the authenticity of our vocation. They serve as guideposts as we move along our prayer path. The more we encounter these images and characteristics of God in our life, the more we can be assured that the Spirit is pointing us to God's direction.

Constants in God's Call:

• God calls us in a personal manner.
• The God who calls us is ever faithful. God has known and has loved us for all eternity.
• God always takes the initiative.
• God is the One who provides us with the grace to respond with generous hearts in order that we may learn "to give without counting the cost."

• God calls us to mirror the Divine Life in us through a life of simplicity.

• God educates us to trust, love, hope so that we may be fruitful.

• God takes no notice of our human qualities. Instead, God reckons with what is nothing and worthless to humble those who believe only in their own powers and riches.

• God calls us to something difficult. The mission itself entails hardships and sacrifices, but the Divine presence and assurance are always there.

•When God calls, the one called from among the people, is to serve them.

• God calls us to bring the Good News to the poor.

•Those who are called cannot remain indifferent. Awareness of one's vocation goes deeper than one's limitations and shortcomings.

•Those who have responded have had fears and doubts. They were aware of the greatness of their mission and their human weakness. They ended by giving themselves over completely to God, the ever-faithful One.

Each succeeding chapter therefore begins with one of the constants as a point for prayerful consideration. It serves as a backdrop for the Scripture meditations that follow. Reflection questions are also offered. These may or may not be used depending on the Spirit's inspiration. Additional Biblical passages are also given as optional suggestions for meditation.

Each chapter may be used as a theme for a day of recollection or for each day of a guided retreat. The other Scripture suggestions may be used as optional materials.

For group retreats or recollection, the reflection questions may be used as guides for the group's faith-sharing. Again, the use of these questions is optional.

Suggestions for Using the Scripture Meditations

1. Preparation for the day:

   Read *Point for Prayerful Consideration* and the brief notes on the theme.

2. Immediate preparation for prayer:
   a) Relax and quiet my self.
   b) Recall the *point for prayerful consideration.*
   c) Ask for the grace to be open and to be responsive to God's word.
   d) Read the Scripture passage and the guiding notes.

3. Entering into Prayer: Allow God's word to take root in my heart. *Listen openly* to the Word, *interact honestly* with the Lord, *wait patiently* for the Spirit's leading, and *trust humbly* in God.

4. End the prayer period with thanksgiving.

5. After the prayer period, journal the prayer. What happened during the period of prayer? How did I experience God? What were my feelings? What stirred within me? (One or two of the reflection questions may be used, if helpful.)

Invitation and Promise

Point for prayerful consideration: *God calls us in a personal manner.*

Brief Notes on the Theme:

In calling us by name, God awakens us to our true selves, giving us a sense of *identity* — who and what we are before God. Yet, this identity is always within the context of a *community* of persons in which we feel a sense of belonging.

We are born into a human family. We grow as we learn to relate with others and with our world. In our relationships, we discover that our actions, reactions or non-actions affect one another and the quality of life we are all meant to live. We feel a *sense of responsibility* not only for our own destiny but for the destiny of others. Only when we have responded to what God is offering us and have acted responsibly towards life, do we receive a *sense of dignity* as persons.

Identity, community, responsibility, and dignity — these are all part of God's promise to each of us as we listen to the voice of divine invitation.

Scripture Meditation #1

Genesis 12:1-5... *"In you all people of the earth will be blessed. I will make your name great."*

Guiding Notes

God's words to Abraham sound more like a command than an invitation. Abraham is being asked to abandon *all* his sources of identity and security — his country, family, and home — for a place God will show him.

What impelled Abraham to respond in faith? What is in God's promise that made Abraham abandon all and follow a life of utter insecurity?

God promises Abraham to make him a great nation, to bless him and to make his name great. As we look more closely at God's promise, we see the attractiveness of it. When a nation is great, its citizens feel a great sense of pride and dignity in their being part of it. That nation's founding mother or father is in turn considered great — her or his name respected, honored and remembered by present and future generations.

As an old man, Abraham is as good as dead, for he has no sons to bear his name, a name that will be carried with pride by his children and his children's children. Therefore, God's call fills him with hope that life will spring forth from his sterile relationship with Sarah. Out of their nothingness comes a new beginning.

Reflection Questions

a) Abraham's life is a paradigm of what it means to be a person of faith. In what ways does this text speak to me?

b) What are the sources of my identity and security? What does the call to "leave country, family and home" represent for me?

c) How do God's promises speak to me in my situation?

d) What are my feelings and realizations?

Scripture Meditation #2

Exodus 3:1-12... *"Moses! Moses! Go now...I am sending you to bring my people out of Egypt...I will be with you."*

Guiding Notes

God calls Moses at a time in his life when he had already settled down to a quiet life — with a family of his own and an occupation. In Midian, far away from the sufferings and misfortunes of his people in Egypt, he was living an ordinary life — each day pasturing his father-in-law's sheep.

Paradoxically, the farther away Moses leads his sheep, the closer he comes to God's holy place — the mountain of Horeb. There, God breaks through the ordinariness and routine of his life. God calls out Moses' name from the middle of the burning bush. (In the Old Testament, fire is one of the manifestations of God's presence.) The only way Moses could approach God's presence is by "taking off his sandals." This action is symbolic of how we must approach God in prayer — by first stripping ourselves of our anxious concerns, worries, self-centered desires and ambitions which block our way to God. Only when we have done so can we be awakened to our true mission in life, as Moses was awakened to his mission to lead his people out of Egypt.

God's promise of presence to Moses endures for all generation. God is with us always as our source of strength and confidence in living our vocation.

Reflection Questions

a) In what ways does Moses' call speak to me?

b) Am I allowing God to break through the routine of my everyday life? How do I experience God's presence in my everyday life?

c) What are the self-centered desires and concerns that I must divest myself in order to hear God's call?

d) What are my feelings and realizations?

Scripture Meditation #3

Mark 10:28-31... *"Whoever has left house or brothers or sisters, or father or mother, or children, or lands for my sake and for the Gospel will not lose his (her) reward."*

Guiding Notes

Jesus' promise to his disciples echoes Yahweh's promise to Abraham. Abraham abandons all for the land God was showing him. Jesus' disciples give up everything for the sake of Jesus and the Gospel. Thus, the disciples' call is, first of all, a response and commitment to the person of Jesus and to his mission — a relationship that is more personal and interpersonal than that of Abraham and Moses to Yahweh.

What is Jesus' promise to those who make the supreme sacrifice? A hundredfold! The one who offers oneself in service for the Kingdom will not only find happiness but friendships and many unexpected blessings as well.

Reflection Questions

a) In what ways does this Scripture passage speak to me?

b) What do I have to give up in order to commit myself to Christ and his mission?

c) In what ways am I experiencing Jesus' promise of a hundredfold?

d) What are my feelings and realizations?

Other Scripture Suggestions

- **Isaiah 43:1-4...** "I have called you by your name, you are mine..."

- **Isaiah 49:1-7...** "Yahweh called me from my mother's womb."

- **Joshua 1:1-7...** "I will be with you as I was with Moses..."

- **Hosea 2:16-25...** "So I am going to allure her, lead her once more into the desert where I can speak to her heart."

- **Matthew 1:20-25...** "An angel of the Lord appeared to him in a dream and said, 'Joseph... do not be afraid to take Mary as your wife.'"

- **Revelations 3:20-22...** "If anyone hears my call and opens the door, I will come in to him and have supper with him, and he with me."

Love and Faithfulness

Point for prayerful consideration: *The God who calls us is ever faithful. God has known and has loved us for all eternity.*

Brief Notes on the Theme:

God created us because of love and this love is manifested in God's faithfulness to us. This is the underlying story behind every book of the Bible.

But, like the people in the Old Testament, we are not always able to respond to God's love. We are often stiff-necked people. We are prone to forget God and turn to other gods instead. Our sufferings which we wrongfully interpret as God's punishment often come from our own hardness of heart and our stubborn insistence to follow our egotistic ways.

Yet, inspite of our sinfulness, God continues to love us and show us mercy. God is ever faithful. Every word that comes from God is always fulfilled.

Scripture Meditation #1

Psalm 139... *"O Lord, you know me; you have scrutinized me."*

Guiding Notes

This poem expresses the psalmist's prayer of awe and wonder at God's thorough knowledge of us. Every thing and every creature are exposed and open to God's sight.

God's love and faithfulness are manifested in being near to us — shielding and protecting us from harm, guiding us wherever we might go, forming our inmost being, creating us in our mother's womb, and being present to us in our joys, hopes, confusions, sorrows and depressions.

Though God's thoughts are beyond our grasp, God knows us and are closer to us than we are to ourselves.

Reflection Questions

a) In what ways does this psalm speak to me?

b) How do I experience God's nearness? God's faithfulness?

c) What are my feelings and realizations?

Scripture Meditation #2

Romans 8:28-39... *"Who can separate us from the love of God?..."*

Guiding Notes

God is present in all the events and happenings of our life. God is the One who chooses us and calls us, but we only discover this call as we engage ourselves with life itself.

This passage emphasizes God's all-encompassing knowledge of us. From the beginning of the world God has known us in Christ. God has known and loved us from the very moment of our creation.

However, human suffering and evil can sometimes make us feel alienated from God and from our true selves. Yet, Paul reminds us that nothing can really separate us from the love of God in Christ Jesus.

Reflection Questions

a) In what ways does this text speak to me?

b) What particular circumstances and experiences tend to alienate me from God and from my true self?

c) What draws me closer to God?

d) What are my feelings and realizations?

Scripture Meditation #3

2 Thessalonians 2:13-17... *"For God chose you from the beginning that you be saved through true faith and be made holy by the Spirit..."*

Guiding Notes

It is important for us to keep in mind that it is God who has chosen us and not the other way around. God calls us through the Gospel for the following purposes:

• to save us through true faith

• to make us whole and holy by the Spirit, and

• to share the glory of Christ Jesus, our Lord.

St. Paul, in this passage, recommends the kind of response one must give to God's call — *to stand firm and hold on to the traditions or teachings of the Church which the apostles had learned from Jesus himself.*

Jesus taught his apostles a certain way of praying, of doing and of living in fellowship with one another. These are the traditions and teachings which the apostles preserved in the Church.

Reflection Questions

a) In what ways does this Scripture text speak to me?

b) How can I experience God's call through the Gospel?

c) What does "holding on to the tradition" mean to me in my present situation?

d) What are my feelings and realizations?

Other Scripture Suggestions

- **Psalm 103...** "God redeems my life from destruction...crowns me with love and compassion."

- **Isaiah 49:13-15...** "Can a woman forget the baby at her breast? Though she may forget, I will never forget you."

- **Ephesians 2:7-10...** "What we are in God's work..."

- **2 Corinthians 5:14-19...** "Indeed the love of Christ holds us and we realize that if he died for all, all have died..."

- **2 Timothy 2:11-13...** "If we are unfaithful, he remains faithful for he cannot deny himself."

- **Ezekiel 34:11-16...** "I myself will care for my sheep and watch over them..."

- **1 Corinthians 1:2-9...** "The faithful God will not fail you after calling you to this fellowship with...Christ Jesus, our Lord..."

Divine Initiative

Point for prayerful consideration: *God always takes the initiative.*

Brief Notes on the Theme:

As I mentioned earlier, the first act of prayer is God's, not ours. In like manner, it is God who calls, not ourselves nor any other human being, although God may use other persons as instruments to invite us to listen.

God's initiative manifests itself in different forms. Occasionally, God instills within us a desire and longing for meaning in our lives. At other times, God gives us a feeling of love and responsibility for other people, especially the poor and the marginalized. Whatever may be God's way of calling us, one thing is certain — it is the Spirit who stirs in us a desire to look for God and respond to the call. It is God's Spirit who operates, however unrecognized, at every moment of our life and in all the circumstances of our personal history, leading us to where we are meant to be.

The Spirit we await in prayer is constantly coming in our life, constantly calling us to move into the future, as we continue to journey towards God.

Scripture Meditation #1

John 1:35-41... *"Come and see..."*

Guiding Notes

In this passage, John the Baptist affirms to his followers that there is one among them whom they do not know. As Jesus walks by, the Baptist looks at him and says, "There is the Lamb of God." On hearing this, Andrew and John followed Jesus. He turned around and asked them, "What are you looking for?"

This is a question Jesus asks us time and time again as we go about our lives. What are our attractions, inner dispositions and inclinations? What are we seeking in life? We will surely gain nothing through finding Christ unless we are willing to submit ourselves to him.

Reflection Questions

a) In what ways does this text speak to me?

b) What am I looking for in life? In Jesus?

c) What are my inner dispositions and inclinations?

d) What are my feelings and realizations?

Scripture Meditation # 2

Mark 3:13-15... *"Then Jesus went up into the hill country and called those he wanted and they came to him."*

Guiding Notes

Jesus takes the initiative in choosing those whom he wants to be his companions. They came to him in freedom. Jesus entered into relationship with each one of them in varying degrees of intimacy. In calling us, God wants us to take part in Christ's mission just as the apostles did.

Jesus came in order to save all, but his work began with the poor. Although he himself came from the middle-class of his time, country, and culture, he did not exclusively belong to the poor nor to the rich. However, in calling his apostles from among the common and ordinary people, he located himself within a specific milieu and social class.

Reflection Questions

a) In what ways does this passage speak to me?

b) How am I experiencing Jesus' call to follow him?

c) What do I see as the obstacles to my participation in Christ's mission?

d) What are my feelings and realizations?

Scripture Meditation #3

Acts 13:2-4... *"Set Barnabas and Paul apart and send them.. "*

Guiding Notes

It was during their prayer and fasting that the Holy Spirit acted in the lives of Paul and Barnabas — setting them apart for God's mission.

Sometimes, the Holy Spirit cannot act in our lives unless we properly dispose ourselves to the Divine action through prayer and fasting. Fasting cleanses our whole being of selfish concerns and prepares our inner selves to encounter God in prayer in all the circumstances of our lives. Prayer and fasting create an inner space in us and tree us to allow the Spirit of God to take the initiative in our lives.

Reflection Questions

a) In what ways does this passage speak to me?

b) How have I experienced the action of the Holy Spirit in my life?

c) What is my experience of prayer and fasting, particularly in connection with my vocational search? What particular forms of prayer and fasting do I find helpful?

d) What are my feelings and realizations?

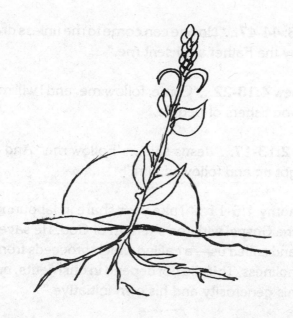

Other Scripture Suggestions

- **1 Samuel 3:1-20**..."'Samuel! Samuel!' And Samuel answered, 'Speak, for your servant hears.'"

- **John 15:16**..."You did not choose me, it was I who chose you."

- **John 6: 44-47**..."No one can come to me unless drawn by the Father who sent me."

- **Matthew 4:18-22**..."Come, follow me, and I will make you fishers of people."

- **Mark 2:13-17**..."Jesus said..., 'Follow me.' And Levi got up and followed him."

- **2 Timothy 1:6-11**..."Take your share in labouring for the Gospel with the strength of God. He saved us and called us— a calling which proceeds from his holiness. This did not depend in our merits, but on his generosity and his own initiative."

- **Romans 11:33-36**..."Who has ever known God's thoughts?...For everything comes from God..."

Generosity

Point for prayerful reflection: *God is the One who provides us with the grace to respond with generous hearts in order that we may learn "to give without counting the cost."*

Brief Notes on the Theme:

Generosity is a word that carries rich meanings. It comes from the Latin root word *gener* which means to beget or to generate (offspring). The act or process of begetting is essentially a choice for life. It involves self-giving.

Thus, the word *generosity* is closely linked to the fruitfulness and fertility of all God's creation — for everything God has created is capable of renewing life. Therefore, a person who is generous reflects the Divine capacity to give and extend life. Such a person is unselfish, magnanimous, open-handed, and free from meanness or smallness of mind or character.

The fruit of the Spirit's indwelling in us is manifested in our generosity. Thus, the more generous we are, the more fruitful our lives will become.

Scripture Meditation #1

2 Cor. 9:6-15... *"God will multiply the seed for you and also increase the fruit of your good works..."*

Guiding Notes

In this passage, St. Paul reminds us that the amount of harvest we reap will depend on the amount of seed we sow. The more we allow ourselves to be used as divine instruments, the more God will fill us with the capacity to give of ourselves more adequately and generously. God is the one who loves, cares, gives and serves others through us. All that is asked of us is to be willing to cooperate with God's grace.

Reflection Questions

a) In what ways does this passage speak to me?

b) What areas of myself am I being asked to give more generously?

c) In what ways do I resist the Divine invitation?

d) What are my feelings, images, insights, realizations?

Scripture Meditation #2

Luke 20:45 - 21:4... *"Truly, I tell you, this poor widow put in more than all of them. For all gave an offering from their plenty, but she instead, out of her poverty, gave everything she had to live on".*

Guiding Notes

In Jesus' time, the widows were considered one of the "little ones" of society because, like the orphans, they had no civil rights nor did they have anyone to protect them. People would take advantage of their vulnerability, even some teachers of the Law who would lodge at their homes and live at their expense (cf. Luke 20:47).

Through the example of the poor widow, Jesus wanted to point out to his listeners the generosity and open-handed attitude that is necessary for those who want to be his followers.

Reflection Questions

a) In what ways am I struck by this passage?

b) In what ways am I like the rich who gave from their excesses?

c) In what ways am I like the poor widow who gave from her poverty?

d) What are my feelings and realizations?

Scripture Meditation #3

John 12:3-8... *"Then Mary took a pound of costly perfume made from genuine nard and anointed the feet of Jesus, wiping them with her hair. And the whole house was filled with the fragrance of the perfume."*

Guiding Notes

Mary was sensitive to Jesus' suffering — to his feelings of loneliness at the face of his impending death. By allowing her to anoint him, Jesus wanted his disciples to learn the essentials of love itself. Love impels us to pour out lavishly upon the other our very selves. Generosity therefore is at the heart of love itself. It sharpens our sensitivity to others and enables us to minister unselfishly to their needs.

Reflection Questions

a) What stirred within me as I prayed over this passage?

b) In what ways am I asked to follow the example of Mary?

c) What am I impelled to pour out lavishly upon the Lord?

d) What are the images and symbolic acts that come to the surface as I meditate on this passage?

Other Scripture Suggestions:

- **Matthew 19:16-24**..."If you wish to be perfect, go and sell all that you possess and give the money to the poor to become the owner of a treasure in heaven..."

- **Luke 8:4-15**..."The good soil, instead, are people who receive the word and keep it in a gentle and generous mind..."

- **Luke 10:25-37**...The Good Samaritan

- **Luke 12:13-21**...Parable of the Foolish Farmer

- **Acts 4:32-35**..."for all who owned property or houses sold them and donated the proceeds...to be distributed to everyone according to one's needs."

- **Acts 20:32-35**..."In every way I have shown you that by so working hard one must help the weak, remembering the words that the Lord Jesus himself said, 'Happiness lies more in giving than in receiving'."

- **1 Timothy 6:17-19**..."Commend the rich of this world not to be arrogant or to put their trust in the uncertainty of wealth...Let them do good, be rich in good deeds and be generous; let them share with others..."

- **2 Corinthians 8:2-3**..."While they were so afflicted and persecuted, their joy overflowed and their extreme poverty turned into a wealth of generosity."

- **Romans 12:7-8...**"You must, likewise, give with an open hand..."

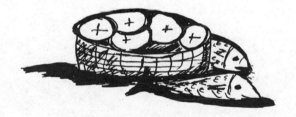

Simplicity

Point for prayerful reflection: *God calls us to mirror the Divine Life in us through a life of simplicity.*

Brief Notes on the Theme:

As human beings, we have the tendency to make life complicated by cluttering ourselves with needless things and worries. We become anxious about so many things that we lose our sense of presence to what is true and essential in our everyday life.

Simplicity is a grace that makes us become like little children. It enables us to be who we are before God — without masks or pretensions. It is a gift that makes us become single-hearted and single-minded. It enables us to recognize and live the truth and shun away from any kind of duplicity. Simplicity opens us up to the spirit of justice, love, sincerity of heart, wisdom and discernment.

God alone is absolutely simple. Simplicity — a moral virtue — endeavors to imitate something of God. The simpler we become, the more our entire life becomes unified around God's love and truth.

Scripture Meditation #1

Wisdom 1:1-15... *"Be sincere with the Lord and seek him with simplicity of heart..."*

Guiding Notes

In this passage, the author of the Book of Wisdom gives us a further understanding of simplicity of heart. Those gifted with this attitude are able to find God. They neither challenge nor distrust God. Indeed, such an attitude is a sign of wisdom — of the Holy Spirit's indwelling. It is the Holy Spirit who instructs them to follow always the way of truth.

Reflection Questions

a) In what ways does this passage speak to me?

b) In what ways am I invited to live my life with simplicity of heart?

c) What are my feelings and realizations?

Scripture Meditation #2

Acts 2:42-47... *"they broke bread in their homes; they shared their food with great joy and simplicity of heart..."*

Guiding Notes

Living a life of simplicity was the spirit that moved the first Christians. In their union and sharing with one another, they reflected in their common life something of God's absolute simplicity.

There were four simple formative experiences that educated them as followers of Christ: (a) faithfulness to the apostles' teaching, (b) the common life of sharing, (c) the breaking of bread, and (d) the prayers.

The more they grew in their capacity to love one another, the more they became known as Christ's followers. The simplicity of their love for one another became the indelible mark of their Christian vocation.

Reflection Questions

a) What struck me in this passage? in the life of the first community?

b) In what ways is God leading me to a life of simplicity?

c) In what ways do I see the relationship between community life and simplicity?

d) What are my feelings, reactions/
responses, insights, realizations?

Scripture Meditation #3

Ephesians 6:5-9... *"Servants, obey your masters of this world...with simplicity of heart, as if obeying Christ..."*

Guiding Notes

St. Paul reminds the lowly of their nobility and urges them to live with dignity, not with servility, following Christ's example of obedience to the Father.

St. Paul invites us to look into our motivation in serving others. Do we do it with simplicity or duplicity of heart? If we only seek the approval of others, then our seemingly "good deeds" are done with duplicity of heart. Our motivation then becomes questionable for we are only seeking to serve ourselves, not others. If our service to one another is done with simplicity, and not with duplicity of heart, then we will be able to contribute to the growth of others and to the building up of the community.

Reflection Questions

a) In what ways does this passage speak to me in the context of my everyday experience at home, at work, or in community.

b) In what ways am I aware of my motivation for serving others?

c) What feelings, images, thoughts and realizations surface as I consider this passage for meditation?

Other Scripture Suggestions:

• **1 Peter 1:22-24**..."In obeying the truth, you have gained interior purification from which comes sincere love for our brothers (and sisters)..."

• **2 Corinthians 1:12-14**..."our conscience tells us that we have lived in this world with the openness and sincerity that comes from God..."

• **Matthew 10:16-20**..."You must be clever as snakes and innocent as doves..."

• **Romans 12:9-21**..."Let love be sincere. Hate what is evil and hold to whatever is good..."

• **Luke 11:34-36**..."If your eye sees clearly, your whole person benefits from the light..."

• **Psalm 131**..."I am not engrossed in ambitious matters, nor in things too great for me..."

• **Job 19:25-27**..."With my own eyes I will see God — I and not another. How my heart yearns."

Growth and Creativity

Point for prayerful consideration: *God educates us to trust, love and hope — so we may become fruitful.*

Brief Notes on the Theme:

Just as God puts Israel to a test in the desert, we too are sometimes led into the wilderness where we are deprived of our own sources of security so that, we may learn to trust God and recognize our nothingness.

Inner chaos may be our initial reaction to deprivation. In our confusion, we feel our roots shaken. Fearful, we try to hang on to old and familiar ways for security. In this very experience of inner chaos, God leads us to discover the gifts and the graces that are already in us. The Spirit leads us to recognize that even in the depths of our misery God is there. God challenges us along the way to discover the creativity and fruitfulness of love itself.

Scripture Meditation #1

Hosea 11:1-9... *"I led them with cords of human kindness, with leading strings of love..."*

Guiding Notes

In this beautiful passage, God speaks as a disappointed parent whose son (daughter) has gone astray. It enumerates the many ways God's people have been loved. God is the one who taught them "to walk, to ease the yoke upon their necks and to feed them". Yet, they did not realize who is behind all these.

The verses remind us of the poignant reality that no matter how much kindness and love God pours upon us, we could still choose to follow the wayward path. Often, we are like the people in the Bible who act like immature children insisting on their ways. Our setbacks, our failures and fruitless labors are paradoxically what God considers the most suitable ways to teach us. Through such experiences, we are taught to return to God and to recognize the love and the care with which we have been gifted throughout our life.

Reflection Questons

a) In what ways does this text speak to me?

b) How have I experienced "God's leading strings of love"?

c)   What have I learned from my setbacks
and failures?

d)   What are my feelings and realizations?

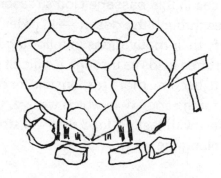

Scripture Meditation #2

Deuteronomy 8:2-5... *"Yahweh made you experience hunger...to show you that one lives not on bread alone, but on every word that comes from the mouth of God."*

Guiding Notes

We see in this passage God's reason for leading the Israelites through the desert — in order to test them and to purify their motivations in following God's ways.

God often leads us through a difficult path in order to teach us to become more responsible for ourselves, for others and for the society in which we live. God feeds us in the journey with lasting food that will strengthen and sustain us along the way.

Reflection Questions

a) In what ways does this text speak to me?

b) How have I experienced the testing of God?

c) What are my reactions and responses when I am being led through a difficult path?

d) What are my feelings and realizations?

Scripture Meditation #3

Wisdom 11:23-12:2... *"Your immortal spirit is in all. And so by degrees you correct those who sin, you admonish them, reminding them how they have strayed, so that turning away from evil they may trust in you, Lord."*

Guiding Notes

This text is part of the long account about God's inscrutable ways — how Divine Wisdom works in history and how God's ways are contrasted with the foolishness of those who turn to worship other gods.

The author, in addressing God in the first person, reverently acknowledges God's merciful ways which are manifested in the following manner:

— God overlooks our sins and gives us time to repent (cf. 11:23b),

— God has compassion on all because we all belong to God (cf. 11:26), and

— God corrects, admonishes and reminds us when we have strayed; so that, in turning away from our sinful and egoistic ways, we may learn to trust the Lord (cf. 12:2).

Reflection Questions

a) In what ways does this text speak to me?

b) How have I experienced God's merciful ways?

c) In what ways does God correct and admonish me?

d) What are my feelings and realizations?

Other Scripture Suggestions

- **Proverbs 16:1-9...**"Entrust all you do to Yahweh and your plans will be realized.

- **Hebrews 12:5-12...**"What you endure is in order to correct you..."

- **Isaiah 30:20-21...**"God who is your teacher will no longer hide his face from you."

- **Revelations 3:15-19...**"I reprimand and correct all those I love. Be earnest and change your ways."

- **1 Peter 4:12-16...**"My dear people, do not be surprised that you are being tested by fire..."

- **James 1:2-18...**"Consider yourselves fortunate...when you meet with every kind of trial, for you know that the testing of your faith makes you grow..."

Graciousness and Compassion

Point for prayerful consideration: *God takes no notice of our human qualities. Instead, God reckons with what is nothing and worthless in order to humble those who believe only in their own powers and riches.*

Brief Notes on the Theme:

The more we have by way of material and professional successes, the more we are exposed to the danger of relying on them for our source of identity and self-worth. William Blake once wrote the following words to counsel us on this human tendency:

> Distrust your heart and the durability of your fame,
> if from the stream of occasion you snatch a handful

of foam: deny the stream, and give its name to the
frothy bursting bubble.[3]

The value of the human person is not in one's
riches or fame. God calls us to understand that no world
is worthy of any human being except one where food and
dignity are given to all.

God is gracious and compassionate to all,
including the rich. To those who have plenty, God takes
away all the benefits and false security provided by their
wealth, lest they are blinded from seeing the needs of
others and their own social duties.

---

[3]Cf. William Blake, "Songs of Innocence and of Experience" in *Poetry and Prose of William Blake* (London: Nonsuch Press, 1941.)

Scripture Meditation #1

Luke 1:26-38... *"Do not fear, Mary, for God has looked kindly on you...then Mary said, 'I am the handmaid of the Lord, let it be done to me as you will.'"*

Guiding Notes

God usually communicates through an intimate encounter with the one who is open to listen and to receive the Word. Like an artist, God etches the divine words in the depths of our being and enables us to respond with generosity to the divine promptings. Perhaps this was the intention of Luke in using biblical words and forms to give us a better understanding of Mary's encounter with God. It was an encounter that filled her with the Spirit and which left her with no other response but to express in true humility these simple words, "I am the handmaid of the Lord, be it done to me as you will."

Through grace, God instills in us the disposition to believe and to resonate with the truth that by ourselves we are nothing — for everything that we are and have comes from God.

Reflection Questions

a) How does this text speak to me?

b) How have I experienced true humility?

c) How have I experienced the visitation
of God in my life? How have I responded?

d) What are my feelings and realizations?

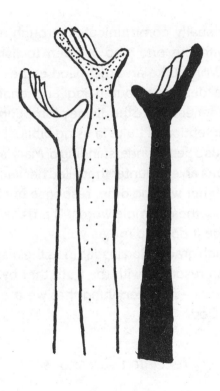

Scripture Meditation #2

Luke 1:46-55... *"You, Lord, have looked upon your handmaid in her lowliness, and people forever will call her blessed."*

Guiding Notes

Mary's Song expresses the deepest sentiment of one whose life has been touched by God's call. One who is truly called by God recognizes his or her own nothingness and lowliness.

There is a time for us to seek truth, to discover who we are, what and where we are meant to be. But, what will ultimately matter is the understanding that God's graciousness and compassion will always seek out what is poorer and weaker to fill it and make it great.

Reflection Questions

a) What word or phrase struck me in this passage?

b) How have I experienced God's love and compassion?

c) What are the ways in which I have responded to God?

d) What are my feelings and realizations?

Scripture Meditation #3

1 Corinthians 1:18-31..."*Yet God has chosen what the world considers foolish, to shame the wise; he has chosen what the world considers weak to shame the strong.*"

Guiding Notes

St. Paul invites us to reflect on our motivation for following Christ. If we are looking for comforts, titles or honors, then we are not really seeking to serve him but only ourselves. To follow Christ, we must not only proclaim the message of the cross but also strive to live that message. The means we choose to announce and give witness to the Gospel must be in accordance with the proclamation of a Savior poor and crucified.

We can only follow the Gospel path and live a life of poverty if our faith is rooted in the person of Christ. It seems much easier to save the world with money, power and influence. Even the best intentioned people seem to prefer this as a more effective way. Those who choose the way of poverty and active non-violence seem to scandalize those who think of this way as ineffectual and slow for the pressing problems besetting our world and society today.

Reflection Questions

a) What struck me in this particular passage?

b) How do I understand the "language of the cross" in my life and situation?

c) In what ways am I invited to proclaim and live the Gospel of Christ in my everyday life?

d) What are my feelings and realizations?

Other Scripture Suggestions

- **Deuteronomy 7:7-9**..."Yahweh has chosen you not because you are the most numerous...on the contrary you are the least.

- **Nehemiah 9:15-31**..."But You, God of forgiveness, merciful and gracious, slow to anger and rich in kindness, did not abandon them..."

- **Colossians 1:21-23**..."God reconciled you by giving up to death the body of Christ, so that you may be without fault, holy and blameless before him."

- **Luke 5:1-11**..."'Leave me, Lord, for I am a sinful man!'...Jesus said to Simon, 'Do not be afraid. You will catch people from now on...'"

- **Romans 5:6-9**..."But God showed his love for us in this: while we were still sinners, Christ died for us."

- **Titus 3: 3-7**..."But God revealed his eminent goodness and love for humankind and saved us, not because of good deeds we may have done but for the sake of his own mercy."

Passover and Life

Point for prayerful consideration: *God calls to something difficult. The mission itself entails hardships and sacrifices, but the Divine presence and assurance is always there.*

Brief Notes on the Theme:

Passover is a leap to something new. It involves struggle, death, risk, danger, change, promise, sacrifice and surrender. Our response to God's call presupposes our willingness to undergo a passover.

Therefore, if our call is to be patterned after that of Christ, the source of it becomes doubtful if it does not entail hardships, sacrifices, risks or some sort of passover experience. This seems to be essential to a true call. We are called to go beyond the limits of our boundaries, to expand our hearts, to forget what the ego dictates and to allow God to empower us and use us for the work of redemption.

Jesus' death and resurrection point out to us the demands of genuine love and of ministry as well as the value of our own trials.

Scripture Meditation #1

Philippians 2:6-11... *"He emptied himself, to be like us..."*

Guiding Notes

Christ's attitude of humility — his path from God to man, from rich to poor, first to last, from master to servant — is the secret of Christian life. Christ desired to identify himself with the most humble, the most afflicted, the most despised. Such were his attitudes and they must be those of his followers.

To be in solidarity with the humblest and to share with them who we are and what we have is a Christian imperative.

Reflection Questions

a) In what ways does this passage speak to me?

b) What are the specific ways in which I am called to "empty myself of my 'godliness' in my everyday life?"

c) How can I be in solidarity with the weak, the poor, and the marginalized?

d) What are my feelings and realizations?

Scripture Meditation #2

John 12:23-26... *"Unless the grain of wheat falls to the earth and dies, it remains alone; but if it dies, it produces much fruit."*

Guiding Notes

Jesus' own passover — his death and resurrection — teaches us the meaning of our own life: the more we give of ourselves to others, the more we shall find life. The more we die to our selfish ambitions, the more God can use us as instruments of the Divine life for others.

Reflection Questions

a) In what ways does this Scripture text strike me?

b) How do I experience the paschal mystery — the 'dying' and the 'rising' to new life in my everyday circumstances?

c) What are the ways in which I experience my own 'passover'?

d) What are my feelings and realizations?

Scripture Meditation #3

Matthew 16:24-26... *"If you want to follow me, deny yourself, take up your cross and follow in my steps."*

Guiding Notes

Jesus sets before us the principle of discipleship — the more concerned we are with our egos, the lesser are our chances of truly finding ourselves. When we are so wrapped up with ourselves, we become prisoners of our own needs and desires.

To follow Christ, we must therefore deny the dictates of our own ego, take up the challenge and demands of a Christian life and live according to the Gospel imperative.

Reflection Questions

a) What struck me in this familiar Gospel passage?

b) What are the concrete ways in which Christ is inviting me to follow in his steps?

c) What are my responses?

d) What are my feelings and realizations?

Other Scripture Suggestions

- **Genesis 22:1-19...**"Take your son, your only son, Isaac, whom you love...and offer him as a burnt offering."

- **Isaiah 50:4-9...**"The Lord Yahweh has given me a disciple's tongue, that I may know to speak the word that will sustain the weary. "

- **Luke 9:57-61...**The cost of following Jesus.

- **Luke 14:25-35...**"If you come to me, without giving up your love for your father and mother...you cannot be my disciple..."

- **John 15:18-19...**"If the world hates you, remember that the world hated me before you."

Apostolic Service

Point for Prayerful Consideration: *When God calls, the one called from among the people, is to serve them.*

Brief Notes on the Theme

One's motive for choosing the priesthood or religious life is suspect if one does not have any inclination for apostolic service.

Apostolic service means our participation in Christ's redemptive work. It challenges us to make the Gospel truly the Good News — the Gospel which brings about healing and wholeness for the human person and liberation from his or her religious, political and social prejudices.

An authentic religious vocation is not for the benefit only of the one called. One's vocation is principally for the benefit of others, especially the poor, the marginalized and the disenfranchised, so that the Good News may comfort them and restore their dignity.

Scripture Meditation #1

Jeremiah 1:4-10... *"Before you were born I set you apart, and appointed you a prophet to the nations!"*

Guiding Notes

God's words to Jeremiah are also meant for us. They urge us to realize that whatever we have received from the Lord is not meant for us alone but for others. Whatever we have by way of gifts, talents and capacities did not originate from us. God has given them to us; so that, we may not only act with love, justice and generosity toward God's people, but work to uproot and pull down unjust structures, destroy and overthrow sources of oppression, and give witness to the creative love of God which can build from the ruins of our own sinfulness and nothingness.

Reflection Questions

a) How did the Scripture text strike me?

b) In what ways do I show my resistance to God's call?

c) In what ways can I share in the work of uprooting and rebuilding?

d) What are my feelings and realizations?

Scripture Meditation #2:

Hebrews 5:1-6... *"Every High Priest is taken from among the people and appointed to be their representatives before God."*

Guiding Notes

The idea of the people having a High Priest as their advocate and representative before God evolved during Moses' time. Though weak and sinful like the people, Moses was accepted by God to be the people's advocate. Christ, like Moses, is just that and perfectly so.

As we look at the role of Christ, the High Priest, we see that all the faithful, regardless of gender, are associated with his priestly role. We share in Christ's priesthood. For this reason, we are called to represent humanity before God for we are consecrated to God for that purpose.

Reflection Questions

a) In what ways did this passage speak to me?

b) How do I see myself sharing in Christ's priesthood? How am I called to represent humanity before God?

c) What are my feelings and realizations?

Scripture Meditation #3:

Matthew 20:20-28... *"Whoever wants to be more important in your group shall make himself your servant. And whoever wants to be first must make himself the slave of all."*

Guiding Notes

"What do you want?" was Jesus' question to the two brothers, James and John. Jesus wanted to know if they really understood what they were asking for. They thought they knew but it was apparent to Jesus that they were only seeking the prestige and the honor of sitting at his side in his kingdom. Theirs was a self-seeking motivation. If their request were for the good of the community, the other ten apostles would not have gotten angry with the two brothers. Jesus takes this opportunity to teach them the true meaning of apostolic service.

Reflection Questions

a) In what ways did this passage speak to me?

b) What motivations am I aware of in my desire to follow Christ?

c) What feelings, images and insights come to me regarding this passage?

Other Scripture Suggestions:

- **Isaiah 6:6-8**..."Here I am. Send me!"

- **Isaiah 61:1-3**..."The Spirit of the Lord is upon me..."

- **Ezekiel 2:1-15**..."Son of man, I am sending you to the Israelites, to a people who have rebelled against me..."

- **Matthew 28:16-18**..."Go and make disciples from all nations..."

- **John 13: 1-20**..."If I, then, your Lord and Master, have washed your feet, you also must wash one another's feet. I have just given you an example that as I have done, you also may do."

- **Acts 8: 26-40**..."Philip found himself at Azatus, and he went about announcing the Good News in all the towns until he reached Caesarea."

- **Acts 9:1-31**..."Go! This man is my chosen instrument to bring my name to the pagan nations and their kings, and the people of Israel as well..."

- **Galatians 1:11-24**..."But you know that God called me out of his great love...and was pleased to reveal in me his Son, that I might make him known among the pagan nations..."

- **2 Timothy 4: 5-8...** "So be prudent, do not mind your labour, give yourself to your work as an evangelist, fulfill your ministry..."

Preferential Love

Point for Prayerful Consideration: *God calls us to bring the Good News to the poor.*

Brief Notes on the Theme:

When we see the poor and the dispossessed, feelings of pity, consternation or even guilt are evoked in us. Pity for their miseries, consternation for the structural causes of their poverty and guilt that we have more than the basic necesities of life while they can't even "put body and soul together". To assuage these feelings within us, we might even go out of our way in the name of apostolic mission to give something or do something for them. But, is this really "bringing the Good News to the poor?"

The Lord's command is not to give but to love. To love the poor is to be in solidarity with them and to reveal to them their call from God. To love them means to help them grow as persons so they may overcome their weaknesses and divisions and be able to band themselves together to fight the oppressive structures that have left them poor and marginalized. Through this they can fulfill their mission for they are the ones who are called to live the Gospel and witness to it in the world. They are the ones who can understand better the Good News. It is precisely the poverty they are in that makes them more open to be helped by God. They are more apt to rest their security on God instead of on things. The really desperately poor can respond to the call of the Gospel with abandonment because they have little to lose. They have a freer heart. So if they have not heard the Good News, then we are meant to bring the Gospel to them so they might realize their own vocation in the world.

However, if we are not among them, we need conversion and true poverty to discover the kingdom with them. This is true solidarity. How can we really love the poor unless we have passionate love for Jesus? When we do not, we, therefore, prefer to speak of giving to the poor.

Scripture Meditation #1

Luke 4:16-21... *"He has anointed me to bring news to the poor...Today these prophetic words come true even as you listen..."*

Guiding Notes

Jesus' words and deeds stir people who have become helpless and open the way for human liberation at all levels. Those who accept him find freedom from their own bondage, recover sight from their blindness, and experience justice from their oppression. Like seeds, his words and examples must be planted in people's hearts and the growth of these in them will urge them to work for true liberation.

Reflection Questions

a) What struck me in this passage?

b) In what ways am I asked to proclaim the Good News to the poor?

c) In what ways have I experienced freedom, sight, and justice from my bondage, blindness and oppression?

d) What are my feelings and realizations?

Scripture Meditation #2

Matthew 25:31-46... *"Truly, I say to you: whenever you did this to one of the least, you did it to me."*

Guiding Notes

Jesus identifies himself "with the least of our brothers and sisters". On one hand, we see that there is a mysterious identification between Jesus and all human beings, regardless of their social class or condition. Yet, on the other hand, the "least of our brothers and sisters" — the forsaken, the poor, the suffering, the oppressed and anyone experiencing marginalization — bring a privileged and a more radical presence of Christ. For the face of the suffering is the face of Christ crucified. Do we recognize him? Where are we in our following of Christ?

Reflection Questions

a) In what ways am I struck by this familiar passage?

b) What is my attitude to the "least of our brothers and sisters"?

c) In what ways am I called to minister to them?

d) Where am I in my following of Christ?

e) What are my feelings and realizations?

Scripture Meditation #3

Isaiah 58:6-9... *"Is not this the fast that I choose: to loose the bonds of wickedness, to undo the thongs of the yoke, to let the oppressed go free, and to break every yoke?"*

Guiding Notes

In these verses, God reveals to us through Isaiah the true purpose of fasting, which is — to give freedom to the oppressed.

How must one fast? Isaiah suggests to us the following ways:

— by sharing our food with the hungry;
— by offering our home to the homeless;
— by clothing the naked; and
— by accepting our own kin and not turning away from them.

The immediate effect of this kind of fasting is healing and enlightenment which are manifestations of God's presence in us.

Reflection Questions

a) What kind of "food" or "gifts" do I have in abundance? E.g., "intellectual food" which comes with the privilege of education, etc. In what ways am I called to share these with the poor?

b) In my present situation, in what ways am I called to share my home with the homeless, to clothe the naked and to accept my own kin?

c) What are the ways in which I can help give freedom to the oppressed?

d) What images, feelings and insights come to me through this reading?

Other Scripture Suggestions:

- **James 2:14-17...**"What good is it to profess faith without showing works?"

- **Tobit 4:16-20...**"Give your bread to those who are hungry, and your clothes to those who are naked..."

- **Isaiah 42:6-9...**"I, Yahweh, have called you for the sake of justice;...I will make you a covenant to the people,...to open eyes that do not see, to free captives from prison..."

- **Psalm 41:1-3...**"Blessed is the one who regards the poor; the Lord delivers him in time of trouble..."

- **Isaiah 61:1-3...**"The Spirit of the Lord Yahweh is upon me, because Yahweh has anointed me to bring good news to the poor..."

Freedom

Point for prayerful reflection: *Those who are called cannot remain indifferent. Awareness of one's vocation goes deeper than one's limitations and shortcomings.*

Brief Notes on the Theme:

To be a follower of Christ is to be a bearer of truth. Yet, such a mission is considered dangerous in a world of lies and deceptions. The one who bears the truth is often rejected as the prophets were and as Christ was. This "occupational hazard" can be the cause of discouragement to those who want to follow him.

But, inspite of the difficulty of the mission, the word of God is irresistibly attractive and powerful. It brings with it the taste of truth and of the presence of God in the person's life. Therefore, it is more difficult to resist it than to face people's opposition to it or to be confronted by one's limitations and shortcomings.

God's word which is Truth therefore sets us free from our unrealistic demands on and expectations of ourselves. It sets us free to be faithful even to the most demanding mission because truth tells us that it is God who does the work in us and through us. Without God, we can do nothing.

Scripture Meditation #1

Jeremiah 20-7-18... *"But his word in my heart is like a fire imprisoned in my bones...But Yahweh is with me."*

Guiding Notes

In this passage, God appears to force Jeremiah's freedom but God does it as the one who gives the prophet the very freedom that is his as a human person. The story of Jeremiah's encounter with God's word reflects the human experience of the paradox of freedom: no one seems to want it because of the responsibilities attached to it, yet people can fight for it or even die for it in order to uphold it. True freedom requires a certain maturity that enables a person to accept his or her responsibility as the bearer of truth.

God's word is like a fire that sears within us. Once it takes root in our being, we can no longer remain indifferent to our mission.

Reflection Questions

a) In what ways did this passage speak to me? stir me?

b) In what ways have I experienced freedom? What responsibilities went with it?

c) How have I experienced God's word in prayer?

d) What images, feelings, insights and
realizations surfaced when I meditated on
this passage?

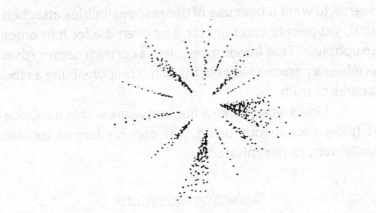

Scripture Meditation #2

John 15:18-21... *"If the world hates you, remember that the world hated me before you..."*

Guiding Notes

It often happens that when a person begins to follow in the footsteps of Christ, he or she meets with opposition from his or her own family or even from his or her circle of friends. The powers of evil are out to discourage anyone who chooses to live by the truth. These powers would want the person to fall back on his or her old ways, to remain indifferent to what one is meant and called to be.

Reflection Questions

a) In what ways have I experienced the "hatred of the world" or opposition whenever I try to live according to the Gospel path?

b) In what ways have I reacted or responded to such oppositions?

c) What stirred within me as I read the Scripture passage?

d) What images or symbols come to me as I meditated on this passage?

Scripture Meditation #3

Galatians 5:13-25... *"For you were called to freedom;...only do not use your freedom as an opportunity for the flesh, but through love be servants of one another..."*

Guiding Notes

St. Paul reminds us that true freedom gives us an opportunity to be of service to our brothers and sisters. He further gives us a simple "rule of thumb" in determining whether or not we are listening to the Spirit of God. The essence of his guidelines is this: what gives life and what does not. Thus, the test of our vocation is our capacity and freedom to say "yes" to that which leads us to life and to the building up of the body of Christ and to say "no" to anything that brings death to ourselves and to the community.

Reflection Questions

a) In what ways did this Scripture passage speak to me?

b) In what ways do I experience the action of the Holy Spirit in my life?

c) In what ways do I experience the opposing spirit?

d) What feelings, thoughts, and images come to me as I reflect on this passage?

Other Scripture Suggestions:

- **Exodus 4:18-21a**..."Go back to Egypt for all the ones who wanted to kill you are dead..."

- **Sirach 15:11-20**..."Life and death are set before us: whichever we prefer will be given us..."

- **Luke 11:23**..."Whoever is not with me is against me..."

- **John 8:31-36**..."You will be my true disciples if you keep my word. Then you will know the truth and the truth will make you free."

- **Romans 6:13b-23**..."Offer yourselves as persons returned from death to life, and let the members of your body be as holy weapons at the service of God..."

- **2 Corinthians 3:12-18**..."The Lord is spirit, and where the Spirit of the Lord is, there is freedom.

Self-Surrender

Point for prayerful reflection: *Those who have responded have had fears and doubts. They were aware of the greatness of their mission and their human weakness. They ended by giving themselves over completely to God, the ever-faithful One.*

Brief Notes on the Theme:

In the Bible, we see that the more God enters into the inner life of the ones called, the greater are their awe and fear of God. From the human viewpoint, their fears and objections are understandable for their mission seems to exceed their strength.

Yet, they ended by giving themselves over completely to God, the ever-faithful One. Again, we are confronted with another paradox in our Christian vocation: the greater the light, the deeper the shadow. It is only in our weakness that we shall experience God's strength; in emptiness that we are filled; and in death that we are brought to new life.

Scripture Meditation #1

2 Corinthians 12:5-10... *"My grace is enough for you, my strength is revealed in weakness..."*

Guiding Notes

There seems to be no other way to freedom other than the way of the cross. Those who are eager to free the oppressed must be tested in their resolve — some through opposition, others through indifference. Often, the source of one's suffering is one's own weakness and sinfulness. This seems to be Paul's experience in this passage. He is driving home to us the lesson that suffering can be a good teacher for it tests the strength of our surrender.

Reflection Questions

a) In what ways did this passage speak to me?

b) What do I consider as "thorn in my flesh" through which the God's strength is revealed in my life?

c) What feelings, images, thoughts and realizations are surfacing as I consider this passage for my meditation?

Scripture Meditation #2

Isaiah 50:4-7... *"The Lord has given me a disciple's tongue, that I may know how to speak to the weary. Morning after morning he wakes me up to hear, to listen like a disciple.'*

Guiding Notes

We see in this passage the profile and the mission of the perfect servant of Yahweh — Jesus. Anyone who follows the footsteps of Jesus is reminded that like him, one will be able to transmit the Word and to give encouragement to others on behalf of God if one listens and keeps oneself open to God's word.

To sustain those who are tired, we must be taught by God, for the true prophet is a person of prayer, open to the Spirit of God. As Paul says in his first letter to the Corinthians, "No one knows the secrets of God except the Spirit and we have received this Spirit in order to know what comes from God. (cf. 1 Cor. 2:11)."

Reflection Questions

a) In what ways did this passage speak to me?

b) In what ways am I called to "speak to the weary"? How am I experiencing this call?

c) In what ways have I experienced my own weakness in my mission?

d) What are my feelings and realizations?

Scripture Meditation #3

John 21:15-19... *"When you were young, you put on your belt and walked where you liked. But, when you grow old, you will stretch out your hands and another will put a belt around you and lead you where you do not wish to go..."*

Guiding Notes

The dialogue that goes on between Jesus and Peter is the evangelist's way of driving home the message to us that love must be our only motive in our following of Christ. Our love relationship with the Lord must be the foundation of our service to others, for we can never love the people we are called to serve without allowing Christ's love to flow through us. He is the one who loves in us and through us. Without love, we will not be able to "feed and take care of his flock."

Thus, Christ invites us first to enter into an intimate relationship with him; so that, we may learn from him how to love and how to lovingly surrender our very lives for his service.

Reflection Questions

a) In what ways did this passage speak to me?

b) In what ways is Jesus asking me if I love him in a special and exclusive way in my everyday life?

c) In what ways have I responded (not responded) to his call?

d) What are my feelings, insights, images and realizations?

Other Scripture Suggestions

- **Philippians 3:7-11**..."I want to know him; to experience the power of his resurrection and share in his sufferings and become like him in his death..."

- **Luke 23: 46-47**..."Then Jesus gave a loud cry, 'Father, I commit my spirit into your hands.' And after he said that, he gave up his spirit."

- **John 6:68-69**..."Lord, to whom shall we go? You have the words of eternal life..."

- **John 10:14-18**..."The Father loves me because I lay down my life so as to take it up again..."

- **Psalm 116:12-19**..."How can I repay the Lord for all his goodness to me? I will lift up the cup of salvation and call on the name of the Lord..."

Appendix 1

Some Guidelines for Discerning One's Call

Some Guidelines for Discerning One's Call

By undertaking the prayer journey, we have come to realize that the process of discernment, though often a struggle, is really simple if we allow the Holy Spirit to guide us. It consists of the following four steps:

1. Be in touch with self.

The first step in finding out whether or not God calls us to the religious life and ministry, is to see God's active presence in our life history. God created us with a certain personality and allowed us to experience a unique personal history. Our personality and personal history are part of our call. Therefore, it is important that we learn to be in touch with ourselves in order to get to know ourselves better.

There are many ways by which we can be helped to be in touch with our personal histories. The following are just some suggestions:

a) I recall experiences, events or moments in my life history — from childhood up to the present — that brought me to where I am right now. I simply recall them and write them in my personal journal without making any judgment or analysis of myself and of my experiences. After recording them in my journal and reading them back to myself, I try to be aware of movements and stirrings within me. I ask myself how I feel about my own history. *(Progoff's Intensive Journal Workshop* is an excellent tool to get to know ourselves.)

b) I reflect on the kinds of things, activities and experiences that bring me life. What are my likes and dislikes, my fears and dreams, my hopes and my interests, my abilities and my limitations, and my needs. As I become aware of them, I enter them in my journal.

c) I reflect on my work patterns. How do I work under stress? To what kinds of leadership do I respond? How much structure do I want or need in my life?

d) I reflect on my relationships. How do I relate with my parents? My brothers and sisters? How do I respond to conflicts in relationships? (Constructing my family's *genogram*[1] would be a helpful exercise in reflecting on my history of relationships.)

e) I try to see how others view me at different occasions and situations — during normal work situations, during times of stress, and during leisure times.

---

[1] See Appendix 2.

As I try to get to know myself, I ask grace from God that I may be able to accept whatever I find in my personal history. I must remember that God loves and accepts me unconditionally inspite of my weaknesses and limitations. Perhaps there are some aspects and areas in my self that I find difficult to accept, much less love. Change can only begin to happen if I learn to accept myself as I am. The starting line is where I am right now.

Another help in getting to know myself is to develop a relationship with a SPIRITUAL DIRECTOR or someone else whom I trust and who can be objective with me. I must remember that if I maintain an attitude of honesty and openness with this person, my self-knowledge will increase.

2. Be in touch with God.

The best way to be in touch with God is to develop a regular life of prayer, not just in times of crisis. A relationship with God follows the same principles as a relationship with anyone else. I have to spend time with that person, listen to him or her, be honest with him or her, and occasionally be willing to wait on him or her. No relationship develops between persons unless they listen to each other. I must therefore learn to listen to the Lord in prayer and not merely ask him to listen to me.

Prayer is my personal response to God's presence. God is not only actively involved in my personal life history but is also present to me through the Scriptures.

I must try to get to know the One who loves me more than anyone does. Prayer is a highly personal response to God's highly personal love for me. Because I am a unique person, my prayer response is also going to be unique. There are many forms of prayer. I must try to find those forms which best express my relationship with God.

Having a spiritual director will help me in my prayer life.

3. The decision-making process itself.

As I become more in touch with myself and with the Lord, I try to gather prayerfully the facts about the decision I am about to make. I consider the alternatives. (It helps to write out the *pros* and *cons* of each alternative.) I try to project what effect each alternative will have in my life five and ten years from now.

If I am considering the priesthood or religious life, it would be helpful to search out information about various religious groups and dioceses, their works, lifestyles, etc. and to talk to priests, sisters, brothers and to people in other careers. I must also consider other alternative life choices which might fit me and my personality. What are the advantages and disadvantages of each? I try to see myself as a priest, brother, sister, lay missionary or Church worker ten years from now, and as a married person with a family ten years from now. Which seems to best fit me?

As I gather the facts about the alternative life choices that are open to me, I try to be particularly attentive to my feelings and to what stirs within me. If I have been open and honest with myself in Step 1, and if I have been open and honest with myself in Step 2, I can trust my feelings and follow the movements of my heart. I can begin to choose what appears to be the best choice for me and what appears to be God's will. There is no absolute infallibility in the choice, but if I know in my heart that I have been as totally honest and open to the process, then I am following the right direction for me at this time of my life.

Therefore I make the decision that seems right for me and I offer it to God.

4. Confirm the decision.

After I have made my decision, I spend some more time in prayer for an extended period to see if the decision still seems to be right. If it is, there should be a continuation of inner peace and satisfaction. This period of confirmation should go on for an extended interval (say several weeks) to be sure that the peace I experience is true tranquility and not just the relief that follows a difficult decision.

Sharing my decision with my spiritual director or vocation director with whom I have worked throughout the process is also part of the confirmation.

Should I decide to enter a seminary or join a community, I must remember that my acceptance depends on their discernment as well as mine.

Appendix 2

An Introduction to the Genogram:
A Way of Reflecting on One's Family

An Introduction to the Genogram:
A Way of Reflecting on One's Family

What is a genogram?

A genogram is simply described as a "completely organized 'road map' of the on-going life in a family across three generations."[1] It is a variation of the family tree. As a structural framework, it enables a person to diagram using both the general and complex information about a family in simplified form and terms. Compared to the family tree, the genogram offers more information. It has the advantage of allowing a variety of facts to be read at a glance, instead of a wordy treatise that would need a periodic review to refresh one's memory on what has been previously learned.

---

[1]Pendagast and C. Sharman, "A Guide to the Genogram" in *The Family,* Vol. 5, No. 1, p. 101.

What is the purpose of the genogram?

For a person to grow in self-knowledge, one needs to understand the significant influences and relationships in one's life. The family is the primary source of this wealth of information.

As a system, the family is composed of members who do not function independently of one another but as a unified whole. The parts are connected by a central sense of oneness, of belonging to one another. This oneness can be a healthy balancing of affectionate connectedness and respectful separateness, or it can be an unhealthy "being stuck together" at one pole or an emotionally distant abandonment at the other extreme. Either pole — the emotional glob that forms when the family fuses or the cold isolation when it freezes — is destructive to the members. "The physical, social and emotional functioning of family members is profoundly interdependent, with changes in one part of the system reverberating in other parts of the system (Bowen, 1978; Engel, 1980; Scheflen, 1981)."[2]

The genogram can be used as a tool to help a person and his or her family become more reflective about their life and relationships. The activity itself can be a "fun" thing to do for the entire family. The very process of doing it can promote not only one's understanding of self but also of one another.

---

[2]Michael P. Nichols, *Family Therapy: Concepts and Methods* (New York/London: Gardner Press, Inc., 1984.)

What are the other ways of using the genogram?

1. *Family Counseling.* Family counselors can use the genogram as a way of getting to know the family they are counseling. The exercise can be done before the counseling session by the family themselves or during the first interview with the counselor. Through the genogram, the following information can be clarified and discussed in the interview: existence of emotional triangles, emotional cut-offs, need for each member of the family to have a differentiated self, multigenerational projection and sibling position.

2. *Family Retreats.* The genogram can be used as a way of strengthening the understanding and unity among members of the family. It can be done within an atmosphere of retreat and recollection. Retreat themes, scripture reflections and other activities can be built around the life experiences of the family.

3. *Engaged Couples' Retreat or as part of the "Pre-Cana" Preparation.* It will help foster greater knowledge of each partner's background.

4. *Preparation for making major life decisions, such as entering the priesthood or religious life, marriage, etc..* It has been established that the Filipino has a very strong "familial self." A person's decision-making often becomes the concern of the entire family. This can sometimes hamper the individual's growth and capacity to make his or her own free and mature decision. Thus, it would be helpful for one to understand the importance of differentiating one's self in the decision-making process

itself. Doing the genogram can help one reflect on one's family life and influences. It can also help the person identify family patterns that are detrimental to one's personal growth.

What facts are to be recorded on the genogram? What possible meanings are attached to or inferred from the data?

The following facts are to be registered on the genogram[3]:

1. *First names, nicknames, and family labels, if any (e.g. princess, black sheep, socialite, junior, boy, baby, etc.) for each person.*

These names or labels often signify the families' wish for a person to model their "self" on a particular ancestor, favorite person, script, or role, or to play out a particular position in a set of family relations.

Consider the various labels, etc. you and others in your family received. What privileges and/or difficulties could have been passed on from generation to generation by being dubbed this or that name, nickname, title or label?

2. *Dates and dates of coincidence/natural crisis and events.*

---

[3]The facts with their accompanying description and questions have been adapted from the article of Pendagast and Sherman, "A Guide to the Genogram", pp. 104-108.

Births, deaths, marriages, divorces, severe illnesses and crippling accidents, emigration, significant events such as building or buying a home, promotions, graduation, etc. People respond to the stress of change in a variety of ways. Review the family date system to see how the family members respond to various changes.

See if you can locate a coincidence of events around: the birth of a first born? Someone's promotion? The impact of a child becoming an adolescent? The death of a central family member? What other events happen within six months to a year after these events?

3. *Numerical positions of siblings (place siblings in order with the oldest on the left).*

The family serves as a training ground for developing social and emotional skills and attitudes. In some cultures, there are certain expectations connected with one's position in the birth order. E.g. Oldest children learn managerial skills; middle children learn diplomacy and conciliation, etc.

What social and emotional skills and attitudes have you learned by virtue of your numerical position in the family?

4. *Physical locations.*

Cultures all over the world have a variety of rules that govern the physical proximity of their members.

What are the rules for physical proximity for your culture? Family? How close is "too close"? How far is "too far"?

Next door? The same town but opposite sides? Within an hour's traveling time by car, air, etc...? The Philippines is divided into many islands, provinces and regions. What were the circumstances of your family's emigration? When family members put physical distance between themselves, they do it for a variety of reasons (going where the work is, health or medical reasons, etc.) Where are the members of the extended family located? When did members of the family move to where they are?, etc.

5. *Frequency or non-frequency of contact between various members of the extended family.*

One can explore further the pattern of emotional cohesiveness of one's own family by gathering information about communication.

Who contacts whom? Is family business handled only at special events and holidays? How do people keep each other posted as to their personal and life changes? How do people make contact: mail? telephone? visits? photos?, etc. Is reciprocity required? suggested? unimportant? Is there a central clearing house that family information tends to flow through?

6. *Closest relationship and most distant relationship on each generational level.*

We each have our own definition of close and distant, which we have created out of the set of relations in which we live emotionally. These definitions contain the way in which we are close, how we expect others to react to our sharing of experience, our problem, etc., (e.g. they should ask questions; they shouldn't ask questions, but only listen, etc.)

With which person in your own generation do you have the closest relationship? most distant relationship? Of your parents' generation? Of your grandparents' generation? What are the similarities in these relationships? What is your style of closeness? of distance? What rules couldn't you break? Does someone talk for you to these people? What is there about these relationships that make it safe for you to be personal? What sets you off when you are near these people?

7. Characteristics of the relationships you form with each person on the genogram (e.g. "I never met them," "person to person," "we hear about each other from...", etc.).

The dance of life moves magically along, each moving toward the other and away with perfect timing. During periods of stress both dancers change their steps as though several bands were playing on the same dance floor.

In each relationship, are you the pursuer or the distancer? How does it vary? By sex? By age? By their being like so and so? Are there people you have a "hear-say relationship" with? (i.e. you hear about the person but don't know them.) Relatives you have never met? Who are they? How do they play a part in your emotional life? What part do they take in the family drama?

8. *Emotional cut-offs: What was the event? When did it happen?*

During the emotional history of most families, some member commits an unpardonable act and no one talks to them, or some variation that creates an emotional cut-off.

In your family, from whom are you or your family emotionally cut-off? When did it happen? What happened that resulted in a cut-off? What else was going on in the family emotional field (see Dates of Coincidence and Natural Crisis.) What still "goes on" that you or the family stay cut-off? What "uproar" would occur if the cut-off was breached?

9. General situational influences:

Culture plays an important role in the behavior and emotional responses of its bearers.

(a) Ethnicity or regional presentation of each nuclear family household.

What values, attitudes, etc., does your culture present as important? What ethnic or regional traditions influenced you?

(b) Religious affiliation and participation of each nuclear family household.

What is your family's religious tradition? How does it influence rites of passage? Celebrations? Values and ideals? Does the practice or lack of practice become a family issue? Early in the children's lives? In adolescence? In young adulthood?

(c) Socio-economic level of each nuclear family household. (Socio-economic class, like ethnicity and religion, has a profound formative impact on who one is.)

What socio-economic level does your income and heritage make you? In the extended family, do the various nuclear units belong to the same socio-economic level? Does the similarity or variety create mutual growth? Are there rules for mobility? Are the resources available to foster the mobility?

(d) Issues with intense emotional charge for each nuclear family household (e.g. politics, money, alcohol, sex, etc.).

What are the issues your parents never talked about? Always talked about with ease and flexibility? What topics did your parents tell you their parents would never let them talk about? Is their position on these issues the opposite of your own parents? Is yours the opposite of your parents?

How are these facts represented on the genogram?

The following general symbols represent the following information[4]:

Male: ▢   Female: ◯

___

[4]*Pendagast and Sherman, ibid. p. 102.*

Marriage Relationship: Parent-child Relationship:

Relationship: Adopted Child:

Pregnancy: Miscarriage or Abortion:

Death: Divorce:

Separation: Twins (this case girls):

Intensity of Relationships: Conflictual:

Distant:

___D___

How to do the genogram:

The following are the general instructions:

1. Begin filling in the information about the nuclear family first. To see definite patterns, a three-generational genogram is recommended.

2. Do the wife's family on the right-hand side of the page while the husband's family on the left-hand side. The father is always on the left side and the mother is on the right side.

3. Children and siblings should be shown in order of age, beginning with the oldest on the left.

4. Age of each person is put inside the symbol.

(See sample of Basic Genogram on the next page.)

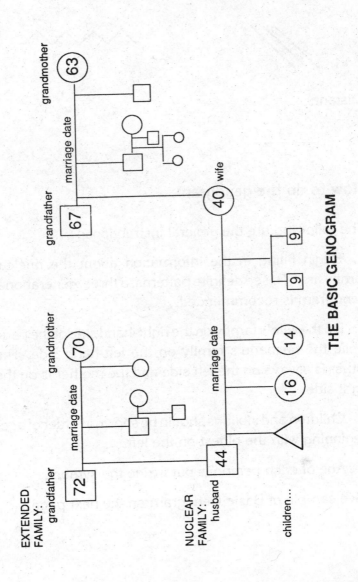

THE BASIC GENOGRAM

Bibliography

A Guide to Religious Ministries (New York: The Catholic News Publishing Co., 1989).

Blake, William. *Poetry and Prose of William Blake* (London: Nonsuch Press, 1941).

Christian Community Bible: Catholic Pastoral Edition (Manila, Philippines: Claretian Publications, St. Paul Publications, and Divine Word Publications, 1988).

Nichols, Michael P. *Family Therapy: Concepts and Methods* (New York/London: Gardner Press, Inc., 1984).

Pendagast, M. and Sharman, C., "A Guide to the Genogram" in *The Family*, Vol. 5, No. 1, 1986.